Girl

Be Your Own Best Friend

**IT'S TIME TO RECEIVE ALL THE ENCOURAGEMENT
AND MOTIVATION YOU GIVE TO EVERYONE ELSE, EXCEPT YOU!**

31 DAY DEVOTIONAL

ELAINE S. BROASTER-WHITE

Girl

Be Your Own Best Friend

IT'S TIME TO RECEIVE ALL THE ENCOURAGEMENT
AND MOTIVATION YOU GIVE TO EVERYONE ELSE, EXCEPT YOU!

31 DAY DEVOTIONAL

ELAINE S. BROASTER-WHITE

Published By: Pen Legacy®
Edited By: Abigail Summer
Typesetting By: Junnita Jackson
Interior Designing & Formatting By: Tamika Singleton

Library of Congress Cataloging – in- Publication Data has been applied for.

ISBN: 978-1-7351424-0-1

Cover image purchased from VectorStock Media Ltd. on June 10, 2020

Interior images were retrieved on May 29, 2020 from Unsplash Inc. and Pexels.com

PRINTED IN THE UNITED STATES OF AMERICA.

Table of Contents

Introduction

Hey Best Friends,

How are you? I am super excited that you are beginning to see the value and worth of encouragement and advice you give others. You know that life-changing advice you give to others but fail to implement in your own life. Why is that? Why is it challenging for you to accept your help? Far too often, we live and depend on others to validate who we are when we have everything we need at our disposal. However, as women, we are nurturers by nature, thus causing us to uplift, build, and encourage others while having difficulties taking our advice and wisdom. If you're like me, you look the part, though. People think you have it together when, in reality, I fight to get through and, at times, suffer in silence because I often question myself.

Now I know you may be thinking to yourself, "Why is she qualified to coach me through this?" Hold on, I will explain! I hold a BSW (Bachelor of Social Work) from the prestigious LaSalle University. I am also a Minister, Youth Leader, Sunday School Teacher, Speaker, and Certified Mental Health First Aid. I also facilitate Self-Love Workshops, mentor young girls and women. In 2017, I created a movement, and Facebook Group called Self-Love – It's an Inside Job.

I have incorporated my education, wisdom, skills, and passion for helping women, but experience has been my best teacher.

I was in an uncommitted relationship with a guy for 13 years. Yes! You heard that right. I wanted so bad to be committed, though. We would connect when it was advantageous for him. He always made excuses about why he couldn't be with me. Throughout those 13 years, he was in a relationship with his children's mother as well. "He stayed with the mother of his children because of the children."

I felt so stupid! One moment I was mad and angry with him, and I fell for all the promises he made the next minute. I felt less than and unworthy. I always compared myself to his children's mother.

Towards the end of our 13-year relationship, I became tired of the broken promises, tired of the lies, and tired of being treated less than I deserved. I started to reflect on how my relationships mirrored one another. I've been cheated on, lied to, and mistreated. Preaching to the choir, right?

It was me; I did not value myself; it showed up in my decision making. I also realized that this and other romantic relationships mirrored the relationship with my father as a child. You'll read more about that later. I decided that I would set the standard for what I wanted. I began to see and accept myself, flaws, mistakes, and all. I FORGAVE MYSELF! I TRUSTED MY WORDS AND ADVICE I GAVE TO OTHERS. The result of my past made me the unapologetic woman I am today. As it related to relationships, I started making my own rules and commanded that whoever I CHOSE would follow the rules. I also held myself to those standards.

I STOPPED SEEING THIS GUY. Initially, he thought it was a joke. After all, I broke it off before. THIS TIME WAS DIFFERENT. I knew who I was, what I deserved and wanted. I HAD TO MAKE THE CHANGES.

One tool that helped me to overcome was self-reflection. I began to self-examine to find out why I continuously made wrong decisions in choosing these relationships and people who did not value me. This self-reflection led me to a path of investigation. I started from the beginning and examined my life, relationships, decisions, etc., I also considered my background and what I witnessed through other people's lives.

This investigation taught me more about myself. I just wanted to be loved. Can you relate?

Ironically, I met my husband the year after I met "the guy." My husband and I have been friends since 1996. We worked together at a then-popular children's clothing store and remained friends over the years. While we weren't always in contact, each time we saw each other, it was all love.

After weeks of conversing, he texted me while he was away for work and said, "When I get back in town, I would like to take you to dinner to discuss you becoming Mrs. White."

WHATTTTTT?!?!?

I loved and valued myself enough to give this a chance. I made the rules and did not compromise at any point. For the first time in my life, I had been in control of myself, my wants, and my needs. I commanded respect, by the way, I treated myself. I loved myself, and I valued who God made. I realized my worth. It is a continuous journey, and to this day, it has not stopped. I not only appreciate myself, but I also valued the wisdom God has given me. I take my advice. At times you must trust yourself to build yourself up. Don't wait for anyone else to do it. The truth is, you may be expecting it, and it may never happen. In one of my favorite books (the Bible), David encouraged himself when he was in distress. When your world is closing in, and there is no one around to lift you up, you must help yourself to fight and keep going. Girl, clap for yourself the loudest! Be your best cheerleader!

So based on my continuous revelation and newfound wisdom, I decided to pen this 31-day devotional to share what I learned with you and offer actionable steps and practical exercises that will position you to find your voice. The voice of positive words, affirmations, and encouragement will help you reconnect with your personal belief and mindset. Having the ability to hear, listen, and trust your voice, a God-given voice will help you see yourself the way God sees you, which will help you in implementing and executing boldly and confidently. I hope that by the time you reach the 31st day, you will have a clear understanding of who you are and have the strength to accept every inch of your well-being. Ultimately, being comfortable to take and trust your advice through sincere, tough love.

Enjoy the journey, and I can't wait to hear all about your transformation, education, and growth.

Your Sister in Love,

Day 1

Get Your Mind Right! You Are What You Think You Are.

One day while getting dressed in front of my then 6-year-old daughter, I said, "I am so fat!" She said, "Mom don't talk about yourself like that." My 6-year-old shut me down! Her statement caused me to think about a few things. One, I am her example. Two, because I thought I was fat (relative), I dressed to cover up the areas I thought were fat and three, she was right!

As much as we want to be or not, we are someone's example. Whether you have children or not, you are someone's example. Someone is carefully watching you, and what you put out positively or negatively impacts their thoughts, behaviors, and ideas. Gone are the days of "do what I say, not what I do." Some kids will call you out on your stuff! Be intentional about what you say and do. Someone is watching. I also saw that my mind and thoughts concerning myself dictated and still dictates my behavior. What you think you are, you are. My reflections concerning myself led me to make negative comments about myself, and they led me to subconsciously hide those imperfections.

A Message from Your Best Friend!
1. For every negative thought that comes to your mind, counteract it with positive thinking.
2. Surround yourself with people and relationships that will build you up, hold you accountable for your actions, and ultimately reflect who you want to be and how you want to feel. Energies are contagious!

Get your phone right now and unfollow every person on social media that causes you to feel less of yourself because you don't look a certain way, have a particular figure, etc. You don't need that kind of negativity!

Day 2

The Sky Isn't the Limit,

You Are!

Take the Limits Off!

Day 2

The Sky Isn't the Limit, You Are! Take the Limits Off!

How many times have you talked yourself out of a dream, goal, or aspiration? Do you allow thoughts of not being good enough, smart enough, capable, or qualified to distract and deter you? Do you procrastinate? Are you constantly comparing yourself to what you see on social media? Do you look at what others are doing and compare your dreams to theirs and give up? Do you encourage everyone around you to do and be great, but when it comes to yourself, you talk yourself out of obtaining your dreams?

Wait, you even have the skills and what it takes, but you're just lazy! Or you're like me? Do you allow fear to override your dreams, goals, and aspirations, fear of what people will say, and who will support you? Do you continuously have nagging ideas, but you ignore them? Girl! Forget about the Sky being the limit; you're the limit. You're placing restrictions on yourself! STOP! It's time to be truthful to yourself. You can do this!! You have what it takes! Move past yourself and go! Don't stop until you're at the finish line and get in the race again when you get there.

A Message from Your Best Friend!
Google 3 things that have been on your heart to complete and learn more about them.

1. Check out your friend's list, either Facebook or Instagram, and reach out to at least three people who are excelling in the area you want to pursue and engage in conversation.

Create an actionable plan and a deadline in which your dream will manifest.

Day 3

I Am
Who God
Says I Am

I Am Who God Says I Am!

You are fearfully and wonderfully made! You are worthy! You have talents and the ability to be great. When God blew life into your body, you gained a greater sense of purpose, passion, and prosperity. God did not bless you with the gift of life so that you can answer to what the society calls you. You are not a stereotype.

Far too often, we adapt, accept, and acknowledge the many titles people give us to identify our position and purpose in life. If you are like me, I am a mother, wife, employee, entrepreneur, friend, and someone's relative. Even though those titles are amazing and a blessing to have, you can't allow yourself to lose focus on the most prestigious title, which is being a child of God. You are a child of God! You can do all things through Him that strengthens you! You can reap the benefits of everything you work hard to obtain. There is no one like you, but are you living your life by who and what God says you are? Knowing who and whose you are will make progressing through this thing called life a lot easier.

A Message from Your Best Friend!

Write down six "I AM" statements that affirm who you are. Once you write the "I Am" statements, repeat them daily to yourself in front of the mirror before you start your day.

1. _____
2. _____
3. _____
4. _____
5. _____
6. _____

Day 4

You Can't Move Standing Still

Day 4

You Can't Move, Standing Still!

"He makes me sick, why am I still here?" "Why do I keep picking the same guy?" "This is the same stuff I went through in my past relationship; what am I doing wrong?" How many of you can identify with this? Have you repeated the same relationship issue more than once in your life? Can I let you on a little secret? You attract who you think you are! So, it's not them; it's you! You become what you believe about yourself. Yes, they have hang-ups and issues just like you do, but you can't control them. You can, however, make changes within yourself.

When it comes to building a life and involving others, you must first do the work to get in alignment with who you are, what you want, when you want it, how you're going to get it, and why they need to be in it. I have witnessed women jump into "situationships" (including me) and later wonder why they have not built a relationship yet. Why are you accepting a lifestyle that is below par of who God made? You are the daughter of the King. Are you afraid to be alone? Are you determined to have a mate and be willing to sacrifice your soul? When it comes to love and relationships, you must first deem yourself worthy so that the other person knows that they must value you as well. What you offer and command is what you will receive, so we must look within before we can complain outward. Notice I didn't say demand. We cannot force anyone to do anything they aren't willing to do. You can, however, command respect by the way you treat yourself. You can't move forward in anything valuable if your standards are standing still. Do the work and move on in love, life, and happiness.

A Message from Your Best Friend!
Take self-inventory of all your relationships and situationships in your life. Write about one each day and identify how they serve and hinder you. Those that do not help but hinder begin to take the necessary steps and let go of them. Those that have a purpose nurture them. These relationships will bring strength and reciprocate what you invest in them.

Day 5

Love Yourself
Enough to Invest
In Yourself

Day 5

Love Yourself Enough to Invest in Yourself

Are you working in your dream job? Do you have your dream car, house, and credit score? Have you started the business yet? Did you lose that weight that you promised yourself on January 1st? Did you finally get that manuscript published? If you answered no to more than 3 of these questions, then we need to talk.

As women who often wear multiple hats, we tend to ignore our dreams, visions, and goals to show up and invest in others, whether our children, family, friends, or even our church ministries. It seems like everything and everyone can achieve and reach their goals with our help, but we tend to struggle to complete one task on our to-do-list. Where did we get this, "put yourself last" mentality from? Don't you think it is time to choose yourself and finally receive the life you want? Imagine getting off work from your dream job, walking to your dream car, and your dream spouse is cooking dinner in your dream house, waiting for you to come home. Or what about working for yourself and finally serving the world purposefully? I do not know about you, but I dream and envision what I desire daily. However, the only thing that stopped me from living out my dreams was my inability to invest in myself. Are you ready to invest in yourself?

A Message from Your Best Friend!
I challenge you to make a list of everything you desire in life. List your dreams, your vision, and the life you want. Then, list why you don't have it and daily work on cleaning up your roadblocks.
1. Learn the value in saying "no" when you have overextended yourself time and time again. You cannot serve from lack.

Know that tomorrow is not promised, so you owe it to yourself to start today.

Day 6

Fear Has Held You
Captive Too Long,
Choose Courage!

Day 6

Fear Has Held You Captive Too Long! Choose Courage!

Iyanla Vanzant once said, "If you are afraid to take a chance, take one anyway. What you don't do can create the same regrets as the mistakes you make." Sometimes we hinder ourselves because we are so afraid to take a leap, a chance, and simply face the unknown. Often, it seems like we need a full detailed picture of what we are getting ourselves involved in. That would be me. I need all the details. We need to understand "why things are necessary," "what we are going to face," "when things will start to happen in our favor," "how much it will cost us from now to completion," and "if we will get a refund if things don't go as we plan." New Flash, life does not offer you a sneak peek into the future.

Has a fear of your inability stopped you from achieving, receiving, and obtaining everything life has for you? Have you short-changed yourself out of so much simply because you had questions or excuses that allowed you to remain in a life you are accustomed to? It is time to choose courage! It is time to trust God and believe in yourself that what you desire can be yours. Now, please know that elevating your life will have some hills and valleys attached, but the reward of being obedient will be worthwhile. If you view fear as the acronym "Face Everything and Rise," I guarantee you the journey will not only grow you but also cause you to win at your highest potential.

A Message from Your Best Friend!
What is holding you captive from achieving, receiving, and obtaining your goals? List them so that you can begin the process to remove them.

27

Day 7

You Are
Capable and
Equipped

Day 7

You are Capable and Equipped

2 Timothy 3:16 – 17 NKJV states, "All Scripture is given by inspiration of God, and is profitable for doctrine, reproof, for correction, for instruction in righteousness, that the man of God may be complete, thoroughly equipped for every good work. If we go back to the 3rd day of this devotional, we reflected on "I am who God says I Am" and became clear about who we are, according to God. Doing the work within that day is imperative to understand that just like God equips us through his Word to live a righteous and rewarding life, He also equipped us with everything we need to live in abundance within Him.

Have you ever soul-searched your abilities, talents, gifts, and mindset? Have you ever challenged your ability to execute greatness without any instructions? Far too often, we doubt our abilities and justify our reason to search outward to get the help we already knew. Is it because we thirst for validation or bragging rights? The day you realize that you are enough and have the tools, mindset, and experiences within your years, you will become unstoppable.

A Message from Your Best Friend!
Think about why you do not trust yourself with your life. What do you think will happen if you try and excel with the same advice and help you offer others? If it is good for them, can't it work for you?

Day 8

You're Going
to Get
Through This

Day 8

You're Going to Get Through This!

Has God ever forsaken you? Have you ever had to experience what you thought was the worst thing that could ever happen to a person, but before things could get any worse, God rescued you? Has life served you lemons, but you managed to take those lemons, added sugar and water, and enjoyed a nice glass of lemonade? What is your testimony? What have you overcome that you knew should have taken you out of here? God never changes. He is the same yesterday, today, and forever. If He did it once, He's able to do it repeatedly!

I understand our human nature automatically goes into panic mode when things do not go our way, or we feel that we cannot control the narrative, but this is where your belief and faith kicks in. We were born to not only survive but thrive in whatever challenge we are faced. Life is all about perception. How you view what you are going through plays a considerable role in how you "go through." Do not get stuck on what you see, go on what you know! Gods got you. This time is no different. You will surely get through to the next.

A Message from Your Best Friend!

You feel that your flesh is getting weak and the human within is over-powering your faith, complete and repeat, "If God rescued me from
_____, I know He will make sure I walk away from this with everything I need.

31

Day 9

What Would You
Say to Your
17-Year-Old Self?

Day 9

What Would You Say to Your 17-Year-Old Self?

God and I have been on a long journey together with many twists and turns. I believe I have come to a good place, and I hope to keep going because I am enjoying the ride more than ever. Plus, I know I would not be where I am now without all the varied experiences I have had throughout my life.

Even so, I often find myself wishing I could tell my younger self about how life works, about what is real and accurate, and thereby dissolve some of the harmful preconceptions and assumptions I had in the past. That is a frustrating impossibility, but it is worth thinking about. With the knowledge, wisdom, and experiences I have, if I could speak to my 17-year-old self, I would share so much with her. What advice would you offer your 17-year-old self? Use the lines below to talk to her. Who knows, hearing your confirmation and revelation might just heal some old wounds.

_____
_____
_____
_____
_____
_____
_____
_____
_____
_____
_____
_____
_____

Day 10

Why Did You Do That?

Day 10

Why Did You Do That?

Stop the cycle? Break the chains? Are you tired of repeating the same relationship, the same pain, and the same hurt? When is enough, enough? How many lessons do you need to know that the way you are going about life is not working for you? Why do we, as women, feel as though we have to go along to get along? Why do we always think we have to be nurturing and helpful? Sometimes I wished that life, people, and jobs came with warning labels, I would have known what I was getting myself into before I agreed. This way, I would not have to go back thinking to myself, "Girl, that wasn't the smartest idea."

When it comes to life, we must make better decisions, but we must understand why the same situation keeps reoccurring. Do you attract that kind of behavior? Do you appear weak, desperate, or have a common way that makes people feel that you are worthless and deserving of nothingness? When it comes to addressing the question of, "Why me," we must search our soul and discover the kind of energy we are radiating, which causes us to attract this consistently. Before you ask yourself, "Why did I do that," you must first ask yourself, "what was it about me that made me a candidate to receive the opportunity." Once you understand why things are gravitating to you, only then will you learn how to eliminate that question!

A Message from Your Best Friend!
To start this day, I want you to journal different situations that you recently dealt with and answer the question, "Why did I do that?" Once you understand your "why" and "thought process" on your yes factor, you will get the tools to adjust and put an end to whatever it is.

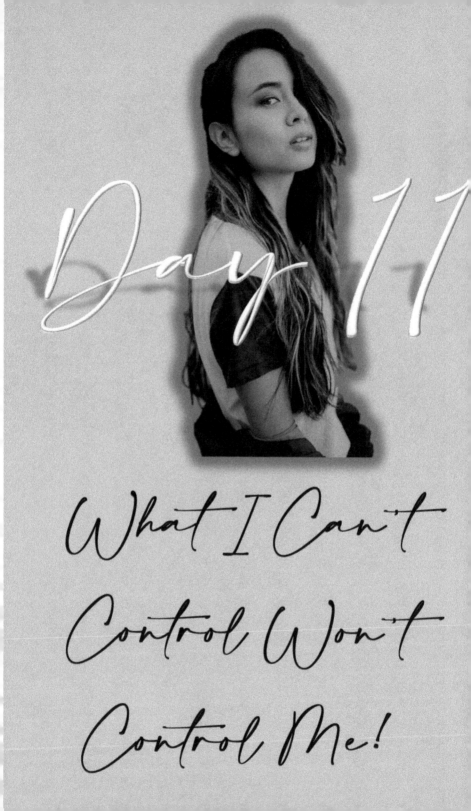

Day 11

What I Can't Control Won't Control Me!

Day 11

What I Can't Control Won't Control Me!

God, grant me the serenity, to accept the things I cannot change, the courage to change the things I can, and the wisdom to know the difference. ~ Reinhold Niebuhr.

Learning how to accept change is one of the hardest things you will ever have to do. Many of us are so robotic when it comes to living that if one thing is out of place or jumps in to disrupt the pattern, we fight tooth and nail with little or no results. Why is change so hard to accept? Why do we see change as something that alters life, when, it's the very thing that will get us closer to receiving what we seek and pray for? Change is inevitable. From the perception of your life to your mindset, change gives you a new perspective on life. Change offers you new outcomes. It gives you the ability to see the journey half full, no matter what is going on.

When you allow yourself to accept change and understand why it is mandatory, only then will you find peace in knowing that your reward is on its way and closer than you think. Again, what are you afraid of? People fear change because it does not offer them the opportunity to know the step-by-step guide of what is going to happen next. You can be blindsided and taken aback. Worse, you can fail. But even in all of that, the change will eventually lead you one step closer to your destiny. Focus on what you can change and move towards achieving that.

A Message from Your Best Friend!

1. I want to challenge you to evaluate your routine and see what needs to be changed. Do not do anything you are used to doing, especially if you know it needs improvement. Switch up everything and reflect on what you experienced, learned, and how the new way made you feel.
2. Set boundaries of change to protect your peace and happiness as you adjust to your new reality.

3. The change should never be stressful, so self-care is mandatory. Begin to exercise self-care and self-love by meditating, praying, and don't forget to get a massage, pamper yourself, and prepare for what is to come now that you have freed yourself from the ineffective daily routine!

Day 12

Do Your Future Self
A Favor and Show Up
for Your Life Today!

Day 12

Do Your Future Self a Favor and Show up for Your Life Today!

By now, you have probably heard the term "showing up for yourself." It is becoming increasingly trendy as a way to practice self-care. With work-related stress at an all-time high and new life-related pressures, we must learn to be our advocates to thrive in peace. Think about it; we spend so much time on 'automatic pilot' doing routine, mundane things, overworking, or doing things for others. Wouldn't it be rewarding to take a break from being mindful and present, caring for your health, or nurturing your creativity and energy?

To help you with this, I am going to offer you some tips that will help you jump start this new journey of wellness and excellent mental health.

- Acknowledge where you are ~ To start showing up for yourselves, you must give yourself full permission to be who you are and embrace who you want to be.
- Notice negative self-talk and make it constructive ~ Change the direction of your internal monologue when you notice your judgments are bringing you down. Try to say something kind, supportive, or encouraging to yourself.
- Create a personal mantra and repeat it to yourself ~ Pick one that inspires you or craft one yourself, which makes you feel powerful and reassured.

Carve out some time for yourself every day ~ Whatever your self-care routine looks like, make your mind, body, and spirit happy by setting aside time for it every single day.

A Message from Your Best Friend!

Get off the couch or out of bed and do something that will not only enhance your day but also offer you peace of mind and a great sense of claim! Your mind, body, and spirit will thank you later.

Day 13

I Don't Care How
Many Filters You
Use for Your Pictures,
You Are Still Ugly

Day 13

I Don't Care How Many Filters You Use For Your Pictures; You Are Still Ugly!

Being beautiful is not just about the way you look physically. It does not matter if you wear the fanciest clothes, high end brands, red bottoms or the most expensive jewelry, but what's more important is your inner beauty; what is inside your heart and how you treat others matters more. Paula Abdul sums this concept perfectly when she said, "I believe inner beauty is beauty in its truest form. When we nurture ourselves, it brings an inevitable, positive transformation." Inner beauty is the most attractive attribute every woman carries. Your true beauty is how you respond, show up, and react to life from your personality to your character. People are attracted to someone who can handle living with grace and class, rather than someone who always has an attitude. Your reaction dictates your reputation, and this will significantly affect your lifestyle, business, and overall mindset, determining the people you attract.

So today, we are going to work on nurturing our inner beauty. It is time to cleanse your mind and soul of all the toxic feelings, emotions, and thoughts that motivate your ugly behavior. It is one thing to be strong, determined, assertive, and about your business, but learning how to be all of that without jeopardizing your "classiness" is what we should be aiming for.

A Message from Your Best Friend!
Answer this question, "What can I do to make my life more beautiful today?" forge ahead to accomplish it
   1. Create a gratitude journal and write at least ten things daily that you are grateful for. By doing this, you will begin to see life differently and appreciate the positivity and purpose that surrounds you.

Day 14

If You're Going to Bring Up My Past, Talk About How I Made it Through

Day 14

If You're Going to Bring Up My Past, Talk About How I Made It Through!

Do you dislike how people hold your past over your head and, at any given moment, are ready to throw it back at you? We all have done something that we are not proud of or that we regret; however, your past does not define you. I often tell people, "You can say what you want about me, just don't leave out the part how I made it." When you learn to focus on life now, rather than life then, you tend to appreciate and get inspired by how far you have come.

Remember that your past is your testimony of how you made it through and still moving through life. Never be ashamed of what you have endured or what you settled for. Just be blessed and happy that you know better now and decided to move past your foolish ways. One of the most significant rewards in life is being able to walk away from where no life exists because eventually, the lack of oxygen will kill you. So, keep pressing and celebrating the mountains you overcome and the valleys you were able to climb out of. Let them talk and continue to watch you walk in your purpose.

A Message from Your Best Friend!
To start this day, I want you to journal your journey of what you have been through and where you are now. Sometimes seeing our progress is the greatest feeling ever!!

Day 15

Forgive

Yourself

Day 15

Forgive Yourself

Can I let you in on another secret? You are human and not perfect! Sometimes, you do not have it all together. You do not know it all. You will fall short of everyone's expectations and desires. I know you just read that and probably wanted to close the book, thinking, "How dare she tell me I am not perfect." Sorry Sis, I did!!!! I mean, if we are honest here, we all can use some self-improvement and chin-checking occasionally. But accepting and acknowledging that you are flawed will only lead you to a life of no baggage, guilt, or shame.

If I may ask, "Why is learning to forgive yourself a lot harder than forgiving others?" We can forgive. But when it comes to us, we tend to criticize and hold that ugliness until it strips us of what we desire and want. Don't you know that when you walk around with all that hurt, shame, and regret, it affects how you show up! You made a mistake and probably a bad one, but who cares. The blessing in your mistakes is that you get to learn a lesson and try again. If God is a God of a second chance, then why quit after the first error? Forgive yourself so you can truly live in truth.

A Message from Your Best Friend!

Please reflect on your past situations and list everything in the space below. I mean, everything that you need to forgive yourself for! As you write this list, I also challenge you to get clear on why you held onto this for so long. Accept yourself, mistakes, flaws, and all and do the work to make the changes, if you choose too.

Day 16

Forgive
Them

Day 16

Forgive Them

Now that you have done the work to forgive yourself, let's address those you need to forgive. Who do you need to forgive in this season? Who do you need to forgive in your past? Don't you know that forgiveness transforms anger and hurt into healing and peace? Forgiveness can help you overcome feelings of depression, anxiety, and rage by helping you make the conscious decision to let go of a grudge. My grandmother always used to tell me, "While you are sitting here mad at them for what they did, they are out living life with no regrets." I know that holding grudges is easy and a defense mechanism to remain guarded to prevent being hurt again, but it is also staggering your blood flow. You wouldn't want this to happen to you. So, my dear, you must let it go!

I know we all hurt differently, and we protect ourselves from recurring pain differently. But what if you realized that they too are not perfect but human. They, also, will make mistakes just as you have done in the past. But most importantly, hurt people hurt people. As it's easy to hold a grudge, have you ever considered having a conversation to see why they did what they did? Was it done to them? Was it a misunderstanding? Is it the only way they could respond because they were taught it was the only option they had? Everyone walking has a backstory as to why they react and respond to people, things, and life in a particular way. But to remove the shame, guilt, and pain from your heart, you must forgive them and move on. If God can forgive us, then why is it so hard for you to forgive them? Plus, forgiveness allows you to take power back over your life.

A Message from Your Best Friend!

Please reflect on your past situations and list below, everyone, I mean everybody that you need to forgive! As you write this list, I also challenge you to finally speak life as to why they do not deserve your power anymore, and how you are now going to use it for your benefit.

Day 17

You Have Everything
in and Around You to
Be Who You Are
Destined to Be

Day 17

You Have Everything in and Around You to be Who You are Destined to be.

Today, I want you to take inventory of your life. From your resources to your network, to your educational and professional status, and winning mindset. I want you to look at your life from the outside and answer me this, "Why aren't you leveraging and positioning yourself for greater?" If you are like me, you are degreed, you have years of experience in your industry, you have friends, associates, and co-workers, and you are fantastic (perception). You have your head on straight, but you are not hitting the mark. What are you waiting for? Validation or Support?

"Grace and peace be multiplied to you in the knowledge of God and of Jesus our Lord, as His divine power has given to us all things that pertain to life and godliness, through the knowledge of Him who called us by glory and virtue." 2 Peter 1:2-3 NKJV. In other words, we're not missing anything. We have been equipped, but we have a choice about whether we will use the tools and resources given to us for betterment. So, if you have it, then why aren't you leveraging it? Could it be a result of fear? Let me remind you that you have the power of free will to do what you please with what you have. However, to be who you are called to be, you must be vigilant and determined to win. For some, that may mean leveraging your resources while ultimately depending on the source, God. For others, that may be taking the leap of faith and trusting that God has your back while doing the work. Faith without works is dead! Whichever is your path, do it now!! You have everything you need to succeed, so leverage it while positioning yourself and win.

A Message from Your Best Friend!

As you take inventory on your life, network, and experience, I want you to list below everything and everyone that can help you elevate your life. Do you have a degree? Do you have access to an executive that can help you get a new job or promotion? Do you want to go into business for yourself? Once you list everything, write a plan on what you want next in your life and who or how you can make that happen with what is on this list! Once you create that list, pray about it. We always want to make sure that our will lines up with His will for our lives. Once He answers and gives instructions, go to work!

Day 18

You Can't Win in Life
if You're Losing
in Your Mind

Day 18

You Can't Win In Life if You're Losing in Your Mind.

What are you feeding your brain daily? How are your thoughts showing up for you? There is a quote that would sum this day up by Lao Tzu that says "Watch your thoughts; they become your words; watch your words, they become your actions; watch your actions, they become your habits; watch your habits, they become your character; watch your character, it becomes your destiny." I can stop writing after that. What you speak permanently takes life in your mind, thus causing you to react and grow based on what you created. That is why it's so essential that you always speak life and greatness to yourself, even when life is not going how you see fit. Your words become the blueprint to your mind. If you are thinking to yourself, "there has to be more in life," just know there is… you just have not spoken it yet!

If you are tired of losing, failing and close to quitting at life, then I offer you the opportunity to change how you speak, especially to yourself. Get clear on what you think and feel about progression and what is holding you back. You cannot win with a toxic mindset. You cannot win and lose at the same time, so it's time to pick one. Change the conversation you are having within yourself. Stop the self-sabotaging thoughts. Embrace a growth mindset by believing that your gifts can be cultivated through hard work, a great work ethic, a positive attitude, and great strategies. You must believe that you have what it takes to win. You must manifest the life you want by acting as if you already have it. Once you mentally see and physically prepare, only then will you win in life and celebrate in your mind. Your mindset is the battery that will either give you life or let you die. It is your choice to make!

A Message from Your Best Friend!

Answer this question, "Do I believe that I deserve to win?"

Self-affirm daily and say, "I Am Enough, and I Deserve Everything I Seek."

Day 19

Loving Me Has Been
One of the Hardest
Things I've Had To Do

Day 19

Loving Me Has Been One of the Hardest Things I've Had to Do

Is it me, or does the society have too many expectations and standards for what is deemed worthy or beautiful? Can I just be honest for a minute? Who is tired of wearing makeup every day? Who is tired of thinking or working to look a certain way to adjust to the famous beauty standards? Who is ashamed to wear their favorite outfit because their mid-waist is a bit heavy? We always encourage little girls to love and embrace themselves, but by the time they are ten years old, we teach them how to hate and alter everything. Why is it so hard to love us for who we are? And what makes matters worse is that we take on the self-hate of what others say about us and fall into depression, eating disorders, or spending money, thereby becoming someone, we won't recognize later. When I was a child, I hated my complexion. I was called names like "darky" and "blacky." Get this, and I never voluntarily wore red until I got older and comfortable with my skin. I let those words from people dictate my liking and self-love. It was not until I got older that I realized that I was beautiful just the way I was. After all, God created me, and everything He created "is good."

As your sister, friend, let me be the first to say you look amazing!! The lip gloss is popping! But seriously, why can't we celebrate who we are? How come I cannot love and be proud of my authenticity without fear of someone judging or ridiculing me. Between television commercials and body shaming on social media, there is no longer a safe place for truth and realness. However, you can build up your self-esteem, self-love, and sense of being unbothered. Loving you should be easy, and today, we are going to jump-start the love train for ourselves. You are your first cheerleader.

A Message from Your Best Friend!

Repeat and complete, "I Love Myself Because…

Day 20

It's Ok to Ask for Help

It's Okay to Ask for Help

Who told you that it is a sin to ask for help? Why do we extend ourselves to everyone but struggle to figure it out when it comes to matters concerning us? Can I offer you a word of advice? It is okay not to be okay, and it is okay to ask for help. Stop trying to live alone. You stretch and bend your life, time, and energy for everyone else, but you deprive yourself of the same help and assistance because you want to be Ms. Independent and Self-sufficient. All of that is good, but you are killing yourself slowly. Is that your legacy?

If you are like many of us, we are considered strong women who have it all together, so people lean on us to help them get what they think we have. From advice to nurturing, we go from coaches to mothers, to sisters, to advisors, and therapists. Draining, right? Your answer is as good as mine. But what happens when you go home or hang up the phone? Do you quickly find refuge from being mentally and emotionally exhausted? Amid you being a superwoman, did you manage to eat something healthy or drink water? The same energy and effort you offer to everyone, I want to challenge you to ask for it back because you deserve it. Start asking for help when you need it or even if you do not. Learn how to take the load off life. Learn how to make relationships give and receive and stop trying to outwork everyone. People will accept what you offer, and nobody will tell you to stop when they are benefiting. If you do not care about your health and energy, why should they? You must make yourself a priority.

A Message from Your Best Friend!
What do you need help with? Use the lines below to list everything you need help with and if you know someone who can help you, send them a text, direct message, or call them. Stop trying to do it all alone!! We are truly stronger together!!

You Are Not Your Mother!

Break the cycle! It is okay to raise your children differently from how you grew up. Use your mind. It is perfectly okay to take what you need during a conversation and throw the rest away. If you grew up like me, it simply means you were taught life a certain way. From our values to behaviors, we were to be carbon copies of each other. However, as the new generation started breaking away from the "old-school" way, they were viewed as being rebellious. Why is having your way of life wrong?

Now do not get me wrong. I am not saying you should ignore the teachings and lessons of our elders. I believe in the wisdom and knowledge of those who lived and experienced the ups and downs of life. However, I am suggesting that you follow your path in life. I often tell people that our parent's teachings of survival are outdated and not the structure of living in today's world. Think about it. Our grandparents and parents understand life as get an education, get a job, build a family, retire, and live until God sends for you. Oh, how I wish life were that easy. Our generation must worry about technology taking our jobs, trying to learn, and establish multiple streams of income, praying that it is a pension and social security left for us, and dodging disasters, all while raising a family. Some of their issues and challenges are not our issues, so I cannot continue a legacy in a world that is forever changing. So, keep the wisdom and some traditions and culture, but it is okay to try living a new way that will benefit you later.

A Message from Your Best Friend!
List the generational curses that you need to break to thrive in your own identity and purpose.

Day 22

The Delete Button Is Your Friend

The Delete Button Is Your Friend

Today is a perfect day to purge, don't you agree with that? Today, I want you to delete everyone and everything that does not serve you well from your social media, to your cell phone, to your email, to your mindset. Let them go!!! Where you are about to go, honey, you do not necessarily need them to have access or a front-row seat. As you grow through this new season of life, sometimes you need a fresh start. New friends. New energy. New vibes. A unique atmosphere that will not only take but one that will be willing and ready to offer you everything you desire.

So today, I am putting you to work. Go through your life and evaluate everyone in it, beginning with your relatives to your job. Understand their value and purpose in your life. Judge their presence in your life if you must. Get clear on why they are there. Do you want them in your life? Are they adding value or being a distraction? It is time, and it's no hard feelings. So I am going to stop talking so you can get to work, and if you do the job properly, you will be left with few people in your circle, leaving enough room to build a new tribe for your new season.

A Message from Your Best Friend!
Go through your social media, cell phone, and email, and delete everyone that no longer serves you well.
1. Go through your house, from your clothes to your books, and donate anything that no longer fits in the new life you are attempting to create.
2. Do a mental check on your mind and eliminate any negative thoughts and feelings that will distract you from moving forward. Only positive and winning thoughts should remain.

Day 23

Fail

Forward

Day 23

Fail Forward

Failure is not fatal; in fact, it is required for progression and success. Failing presents you with some of your best lessons, and it lays the path on how you develop your playbook of life. But when it comes to failing forward, that is where you gain the best outcome and the greatest reward because it strengthens specific attributes that you fail to use initially.

Failing forward is nothing more than understanding how to leverage your mistakes and evaluating what went wrong and adjusting to what should have been done. It makes you analyze, strategize, and get persistent when it comes to achieving your goal. When you understand the lesson behind the lost, you gain valuable information that will help you win and help you rise to a level you once thought was outside your reach. Are you ready to learn and have real-time data on what you are missing or how you can make it better? If so, why are you so afraid of failing? If you want to be successful, you must fail, but ensure you fail forward. The forward keeps you pushing, and that is what keeps you in the race to moving closer to your goal. No one has ever become successful without failing, so why do you think you will do it precisely? Embrace the failure and find comfort in knowing that once you are finished failing and moving forward, your reward will be one that you never imagined.

A Message from Your Best Friend!
Why are you afraid of failure? What were you taught about failing? If you have failed at life previously, please write them below, but this time, write what you learned about yourself and the situation.

Day 24

Don't Rush God:
What He Has Prepared
for You is Much Better
Than What You See

Day 24

Don't Rush God: What He Has Prepared For You is Much Greater than What You See.

Jeremiah 29:11 NKJV, says "For I know the thoughts that I think toward you, says the Lord, thoughts of peace and not of evil, to give you a future and a hope". Many of us try to plan out the perfect life and expect God to bless it. But what if I told you that your life and purpose have already been ordained and planned for you? I want you to know that your job is not to design a new life but to figure out what He has for you and embrace it. Now I know you are asking, "Elaine, how am I supposed to know what God's plan is for me?" Well, I am happy you asked.

The easiest way to learn God's plan and if you are in alignment is by being in regular prayer with the Father. You need to take time each day to devote yourself to the Lord. When I gave every area of my life to God, I quickly learned what I was supposed to do and who I was supposed to be. He revealed to me my purpose and mission, leaving me to learn and execute so I can receive His promises for my life. Now this will not happen overnight. God does not rush our calling because most of us are not able to receive it, yet. He is waiting on us to be at a point of surrender. Once you've had enough and ready to accept His calling, only then will God open doors, shower you with blessings tied to surrendering, and give you everything you desire (as long as it aligns with His desires for you) in abundance. What you want and what He has for you should never be compared, but if you settle for your way, you are short-changing your life and legacy.

Today, there is no message from your best friend because she wants you to use this time to seek guidance from God. She wants you to start the conversation of learning your purpose and His plan so that you can execute, serve, and receive it in abundance.

Day 25

Start It and

Complete It

Day 25

Start it and Complete It

How many of you start and finish every goal you desire? You want to publish a book, but after writing two pages, you find every excuse as to why you cannot finish it. You want to buy a house, but after saving for three months, you realize that you cannot go another day missing a sale at your favorite store. Why are you so easily distracted? Is your brain moving faster than your ability to achieve, or are you trying to complete someone else's calling? You would be surprised how many people I speak to who jump in and out of things because they are trying to keep up with others, or because they want a title without doing the work.

I want you to reflect on everything you have started, from the books to the business or even from fixing your credit to executing that fitness plan. I want you to write down everything that has been started, but still outstanding, and I want you to figure out the main reason why this is of interest. Is it going to help your personal growth or help you brag with others on social media? Once you get clear on your "why," give a deadline to everything that you deemed will add value to your life and someone else's life, and make sure you complete them. Lastly, if you need help, I want you to either barter or hire someone who can help you complete each task you are faced with. The season of procrastination or being the woman who starts but can't finalize is over. It is time to get it done, and the time is now!!

A Message from Your Best Friend!
Journal your progress below.

Day 26

Write Your

Check

Day 26

Write Your Check

Why are we so afraid to ask for our worth? We ask for everything else, but at times we will not ask for the salary or compensation we deserve. I live my life according to Matthew 7:7 NJKV, "Ask and it will be given to you; seek, and you will find; knock, and it will be opened to you." If you do not know your value and worth, do you think your supervisor would acknowledge it? They may or may not. Do not bet on it, though.

When it comes to writing your check, you must first understand what you bring to the table and how you add value to the company's or individual's mission and bottom line. You must look at your performance and your dedication to getting the job done. It is dependent on your ability to continue your education to stay abreast of your industry's trends and loss. How are you showing up for your employer? Because you cannot request an increase if you have not fully leveraged your current one. If you are bringing your "A" game and deserve the opportunity, then asking for it is the only way you will get it. So, evaluate your value and set up a meeting to have the conversation. And if they cannot offer you increase or what you require, then it may be time for you to seek an opportunity that will. You should never accept less than your worth when you continuously show up and perform over and above. What one won't tolerate or accept, another will.

A Message from Your Best Friend!
How would a promotion or raise right now help you personally and professionally?
What is holding you back from asking for your worth?

Day 27

Beloved, I Pray That You
May Prosper in All
Things and Be in Health,
Just As Your Soul Prospers

Day 27

Beloved, I Pray That You May Prosper In All Things And Be In Health, Just As Your Soul Prospers

Physical activity and proper nutrition are two of the essential ingredients for a healthier lifestyle. Regular exercise has been shown to improve your mood and decrease feelings of depression, anxiety, and stress. Proper nutrition can help you to reach and maintain a healthy weight, reduce your risk of chronic diseases, and promote your overall health. How you treat your body can affect how you can show up for your goals and dreams.

There is a catchy saying, "Health is Wealth," and when it comes to executing a better life, you must make sure your temple is prepared to go through what you are about to endure. A healthy lifestyle is the only way you will be able to enjoy the wealth and happiness you seek wholeheartedly. No one wants to work hard and not survive long enough to enjoy the fruits of their labor. So, as you build and grow, make sure you are eating healthy, exercising daily, and meditating to promote emotional and mental health and self-awareness. Feeding every area of your personal life will ultimately help you to achieve every goal at the optimum level and potential.

A Message from Your Best Friend!
Journal your progress below.

Day 28

What's Your

Credit Score?

Day 28

What's Your Credit Score?

Even though cash is king, credit rules the world. From borrowing lines of credit to seeking employment, today's society is becoming increasingly dependent on credit to make purchases, make financial decisions, and judge trustworthiness. From credit cards to line of credit, credit controls how much we can purchase and which of the goals we can afford. However, if your credit score is not at the place where lenders can trust you, it can affect your ability to grow and build the lifestyle you deserve.

If you are like many of us, finances and credit were not adequately taught throughout our childhood. We did not learn how to value money or that saving, and investing was the way to financial freedom and wealth. However, many of us learned the evil that credit can bring when we went to college and started getting credit cards that we could not pay but swiped anyway. We also learned the hard way about credit when we borrowed thousands of dollars to pay for our college tuition. In college, we were balling, but after graduation, we were in for a rude awakening. From low credit scores, denied credit applications, and trying to figure out how to get out of debt, credit left many of us broke and broken. But now that we are learning how to do better, we must finally learn and get our finances in order. You cannot win with bad credit, so get a plan, a coach, and a budget. It is time to eliminate the biggest roadblock to your success.

A Message from Your Best Friend!

To ensure that your credit report is free from any inaccuracies, pull a copy of your credit report from https://www.annualcreditreport.com/index.action and get them fixed.

- Now that you have your credit file, prioritize and start paying off your credit cards and collections.
- Make sure your credit utilization is less than 30%.

Day 29

Pray for Yourself

Are you where you want to be? Are you honest with God about your feelings, attitude, behaviors, and your need for prayer? Prayer is the means through which we communicate with God. It is through prayer that we seek guidance and receive instruction on what and how we should progress in life. You can either pray through words, songs of worship, and scripture. My pastor teaches us that in prayer, we involve and invite God into our lives.

Do you have an active prayer life? How often do you pray for yourself, your dreams, and your future? Or to have God remove those things that are suffocating your growth? You know, you do not like those things but are too afraid to change or do not have the resources to do better. God does not only show up to bless you; He is also available to help you understand what must go. Let us be honest for a minute, what is hindering you from growing? What don't you like about yourself? What are some of the behaviors that are showing up in your life that you are ready to release? At this moment, I would like for you to surrender your displeasure to God and pray for your renewing. Even though God may not solve the problem overnight, He will answer and provide right on time.

A Message from Your Best Friend!

Before you go to God in prayer, I want you to get clear on what you need Him to remove and provide for you. If you are not aware, ask Him to show you. I want you to have faith in your request but believe in your heart that He will answer your every need. Now I must warn you; He may not provide you with the response you were looking to get. God knows your future better than you do, so trust His guidance.

103

Day 30

It's Not
Too Late

Day 30

It's Not Too Late

I grew up without my father being physically present in my life. At times, he supported me, but his presence and money were not consistent. Because of his abandonment, I resented him for so long! As a woman, I realized that I missed and wanted the daddy/daughter relationship I saw on television. However, like many of us who suffer in silence, my father never knew that I held a grudge against him. I never showed it, but he never asked. Until a few years ago.... It was then that I was finally able to share my heart with him, and he listened. At 40 years old, I was daddy's little girl. I finally received what I had longed for since my childhood.

It is never too late to mend broken relationships. It is never too late to share your feelings and pain with someone, even if they have no remorse. At least release them so that you can forgive yourself. As we previously discussed in the "Forgive Them" and "Forgive Yourself," forgiveness is for you. It is in the ability to forgive that you can find peace and the strength to heal. Imagine just how light your body and mind would feel if you let go of all of the baggage, pain, brokenness, and resentment and replace it with all of the elements of life that will build you up!

A Message from Your Best Friend!
Write down everyone who has wronged you and decide how you will let go of that pain. Are you going to call them, arrange a face to face meeting, or write a letter? Whichever method you choose, be assured that your freedom awaits on the other side.

Day 31

Be

Grateful

Day 31

Be Grateful

Often, it is easy to focus on what is wrong in your life. We tend to find and complain over every little wrong thing. We complain so much that we start believing that our lives are jacked up and worthless. We discredit the strides we have made, the trials we were forced to overcome, and the successes we have accomplished despite our challenges. More importantly, we forget that there is somebody out there praying for what we are complaining about. We have taken the blessing for granted because it did not show up the way we thought it should have.

Today, I want you to reverse your need to complain and shout a song of praise and gratitude. Don't you understand that everything you have been blessed with is a gift? You are not entitled or next in line to receive the throne. No! You have worked hard and earned your keep at the table, but you do not own the table and can be removed. Even if you do own the table, a heart of ungratefulness can lead to bitterness. So, I challenge you to be grateful for what you have. Be thankful before you complain and watch how your attitude towards life will change.

A Message from Your Best Friend!

Write down 20 things you are grateful for.

You Made it Best Friends!!!

Congratulations!! How are you feeling after doing the work? What have you learned about yourself? What kind of advice have you told yourself while discovering the real you? For some of you, this devotional was a bit challenging because I pushed you to go deep within to address the problem and its root cause. We cannot heal if we do not understand why we think, respond, and behave the way we do. What you dream of will not happen overnight. You do not get to snap your fingers, wish upon the stars, or say affirmations, and life is all better. You must be your own best friend and do the work. You must be the woman you need to be to save yourself! I hope this devotional gave you the guided conversations that sparked something within to make this journey more comfortable and lighter for you.

Before we say farewell, I want you to use this last opportunity to write a letter to the person you are becoming. I want you to share what you have learned and what you plan to do to execute excellence. I also want you to; *Reassure Yourself That What You Desire Should Line up With What God Desires for You, Remind Yourself of Your Worth, and Give Yourself Some Positive Affirmations to Maintain Your Strength.*

After you finish writing your letter, I want you to place it where you will be able to see it daily. This way, when life gets challenging, or situations arise, and you feel the urge to revert to your old self, your best friend will be right there to hold you accountable for all your actions. Do not let her down!!

Dear Future Self,

_____
_____
_____
_____
_____
_____
_____
_____
_____
_____
_____
_____
_____
_____
_____
_____
_____
_____
_____
_____
_____
_____
_____
_____
_____
_____
_____
_____
_____
_____
_____
_____
_____
_____
_____
_____
_____
_____

Thank you for taking this journey with me,

and I wish you well in your new life

that you are so worthy of!

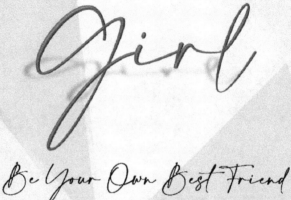

Girl

Be Your Own Best Friend

IT'S TIME TO RECEIVE ALL OF THE ENCOURAGEMENT AND MOTIVATION YOU GIVE TO EVERYONE ELSE, EXCEPT YOU!

Are you the kind of woman who is always encouraging, uplifting building up someone else, but fail to be the same person for yourself? You suffer in silence because everyone perceives that you have it all together. have a degree or degrees and either a stay-at-home mom, entrepreneur, or employee. However, you do not take your advice that you so freely giv others.

In her dynamic new devotional, *Girl, Be Your Own Best Friend*, E Broaster-White provides you with powerful "starting points" for the ne days. Each day's devotion is filled with personal experiences from Elai offer you the peace of knowing that you are not alone. She also incl practical advice, along with actionable steps and self-journaling, that will you apply the discoveries in your life immediately.

It is time for you to show up like the boss you are, and for the next 31 days, your best friend is here to help.

Author

ELAINE S. BROASTER-WHITE

CPSIA information can be obtained
at www.ICGtesting.com
Printed in the USA
LVHW012130240620
658886LV00015B/659